I0815867

Endorsements

This treasure chest of thought-stirring questions posed by Ann Smith, one of the wisest and deepest women I have ever known, stirs around in the dormant corners of our souls, quietly demanding that we come to grips with the vital issues of life.

— **Gloria Gaither**, Songwriter and Author

This question "What if?" is one we all ask, and wrestle with, and yet seldom do we arrive at the answer. In this book, writer, missionary, and Christian leader Ann Smith not only asks the question, but does so with skill, sensitivity, and deep spiritual awareness.

— **Dr. Timothy J. Clarke**, Senior Pastor, First Church of God, Columbus, Ohio

Although I've come to know Ann Smith well, I still cherish the moments when I'm walking toward her in a crowded room. Most of us know what she is going to say the minute we are finally in front of her. "Can I tell you what I'm learning these days?" And the answer is always yes!

— **Marty Grubbs**, Senior Pastor, Crossings Community Church

This book by Ann Smith will challenge you to explore new perspectives and unlock your hidden potential. Dive into its pages and let your curiosity lead you to profound insights and transformative growth.

— **Dr. Lori Maldonado**, Founder, Teach One to Lead One

I have been privileged to serve in leadership positions in academia and the government, and often found that the most influential people were the ones who asked great questions. Ann Smith, one of the wisest persons I've known, has written a timely book in which she asks deep questions which encourage us to understand not only who we are but whose we are.

— **John Pistole**, President, Anderson University

ANN ESPEY SMITH

Warner Press, Inc.
Warner Press and Warner Press logo are trademarks of Warner Press, Inc.
What If? 125 Questions to Discover More about Life and Faith

Written by Ann Espey Smith

Requests for information should be sent to:
Warner Press, Inc.
2902 Enterprise Drive
Anderson, IN 46013
www.warnerpress.org

Editors: Julie Campbell, Robin Loisch
Cover by Curtis Corzine
Design and Layout by Curtis Corzine
ISBN: 9781684345809

Printed in USA

Introduction:

What if we truly took time to reflect and question? We might find new ways of seeing the situations in which we find ourselves. Asking "What if?" has become an important part of my journey, and I am amazed at the impact it has had on me. The questions posed in this book are a collection gathered from several decades of my own pondering and discovering.

Are you wondering what to do with this book? I hope you will find numerous creative ways to use it, whether spending time alone reflecting, sharing with a friend over coffee, or discussing with a group. No matter how you use these questions, don't be afraid of honest reflection—that will foster growth.

If one or more of the questions in this book lead you to a new and beneficial insight, my heart will rejoice!

Ann E. Smith

WHAT IF...

false assumptions create many of my problems?

What If…

how we make the little choices
along the way impacts how
we make big choices?

WHAT IF...

when we form
new relationships,
we could all be blind
for a few days?

WHAT IF...

transparency
is something
to be embraced
rather than feared?

WHAT IF...

accountability
is not just
a concept we
talk about,
but a lifestyle
we live?

WHAT IF...

we stopped trying
to earn God's love
and just let Him love us?

WHAT IF...

the familiar, even if it's bad,
becomes so comfortable
that I find it difficult to let go
and embrace change
and uncertainty?

WHAT IF...

all the energy
used up in hiding
was used for
something creative
or constructive?

What If...

"community" is impossible
as long as we
compare and compete?

What If...

harvesting my failures
opens the door
for increasing
richness and wisdom?

WHAT IF...

life is an incredible teacher,
but I spend little
time learning
to interpret
its lessons?

WHAT IF...

God really does exist?

WHAT IF...

coming down from
the mountain of success
is more difficult than climbing it?

WHAT IF...

I am better known
for what I am against
than what I am for?

WHAT IF...

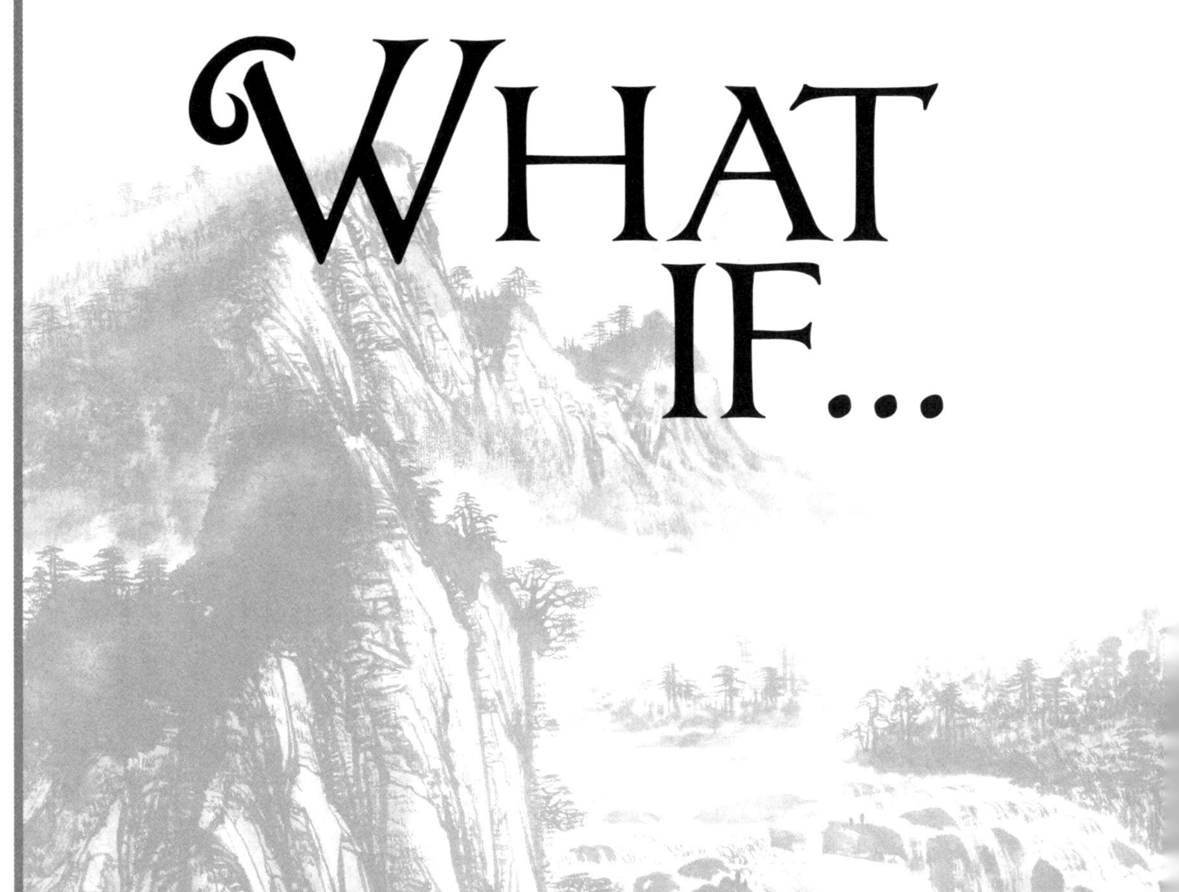

I made a commitment
to becoming
a life-giving person
instead of a
life-draining person?

WHAT IF...

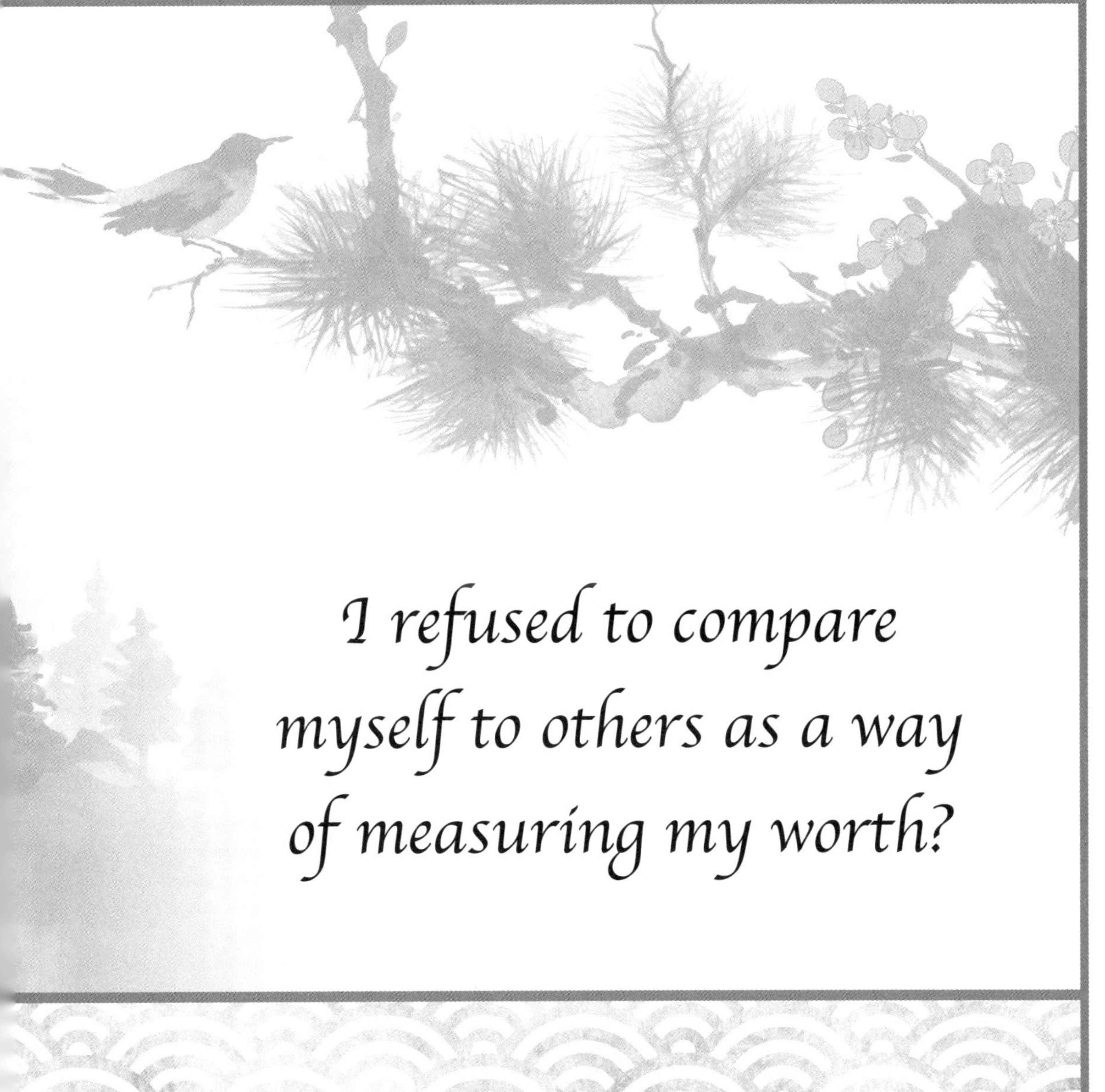

I refused to compare myself to others as a way of measuring my worth?

What If...

legalism is a way
of trying to avoid pain
that ends up
creating greater pain?

WHAT IF...

I could learn to love
in such a way
that differences
become contributions
rather than irritations?

What If...

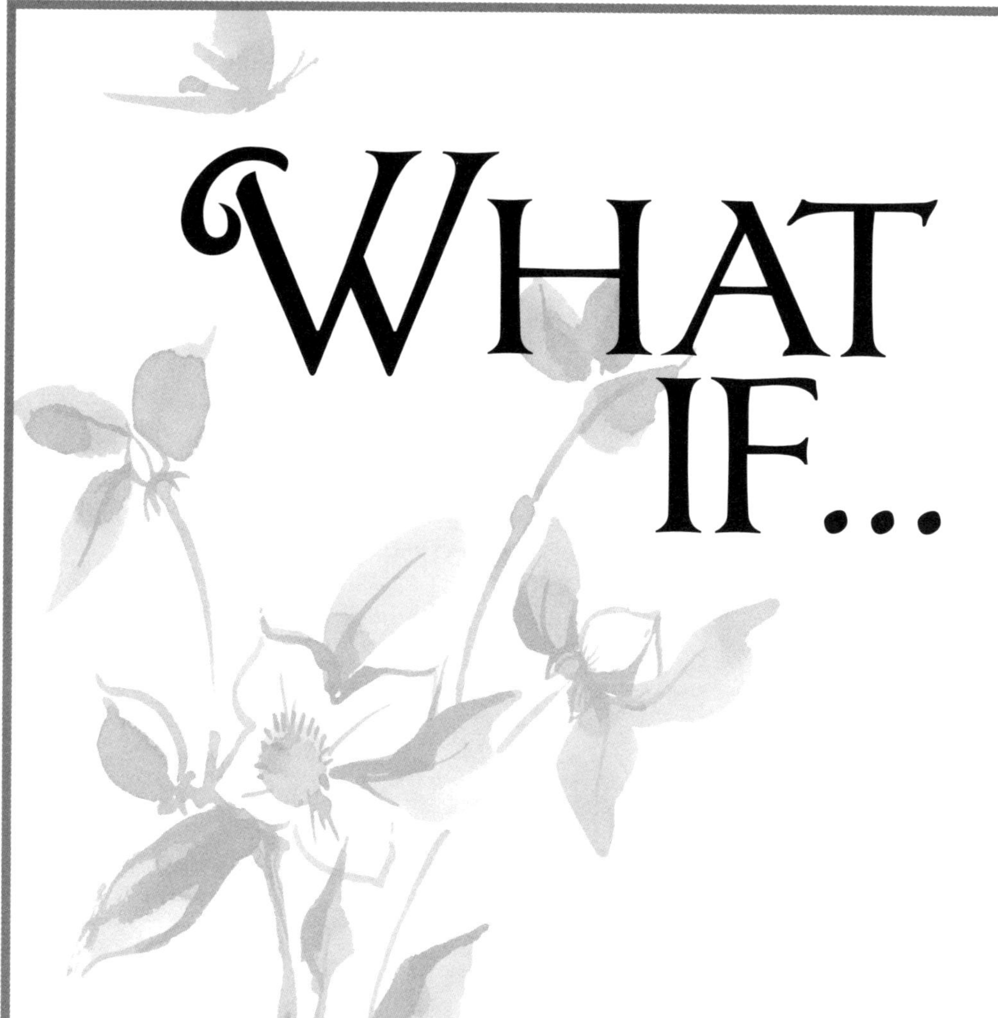

pretending I do not have any failures or weaknesses hinders my growth and influence?

WHAT IF...

my drivenness is a way
of avoiding being in touch
with my inner self?

WHAT IF...

even in circumstances
over which I have no control,
I still have the power to choose
my attitude and my response?

WHAT IF…

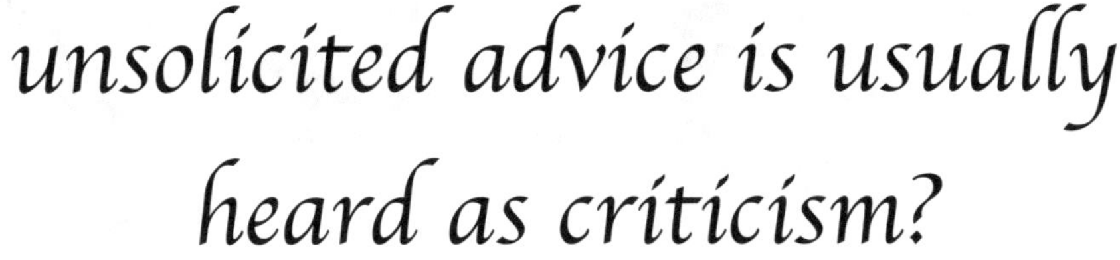

unsolicited advice is usually heard as criticism?

WHAT IF...

I discover that sometimes I try to do God's job?

WHAT IF...

thinking I am
in control
is an illusion?

WHAT IF…

receiving
can also
be a gift?

What if...

the only person I
have power to change
is myself?

WHAT IF…

people who cannot forget
are worse off than people
who cannot remember?

WHAT IF...

*doing the "right thing"
is not enough if it
is done with the wrong
spirit or wrong
motivation?*

What If...

I strive to share my faith in ways that are acceptable to the other person rather than what is comfortable to me?

WHAT IF...

it would be better to lose,
if in winning,
my spirit becomes like
that which I fight against?

WHAT IF...

*when I do not
feel heard,
I do not
feel loved?*

WHAT IF...

I have adopted the culture's idea that winning is everything?

WHAT IF...

some of the loneliest times
we experience
are in a crowd?

WHAT IF...

most addictions have
their roots in loneliness?

WHAT IF...

I could see everything that comes into my life as the raw material for growth?

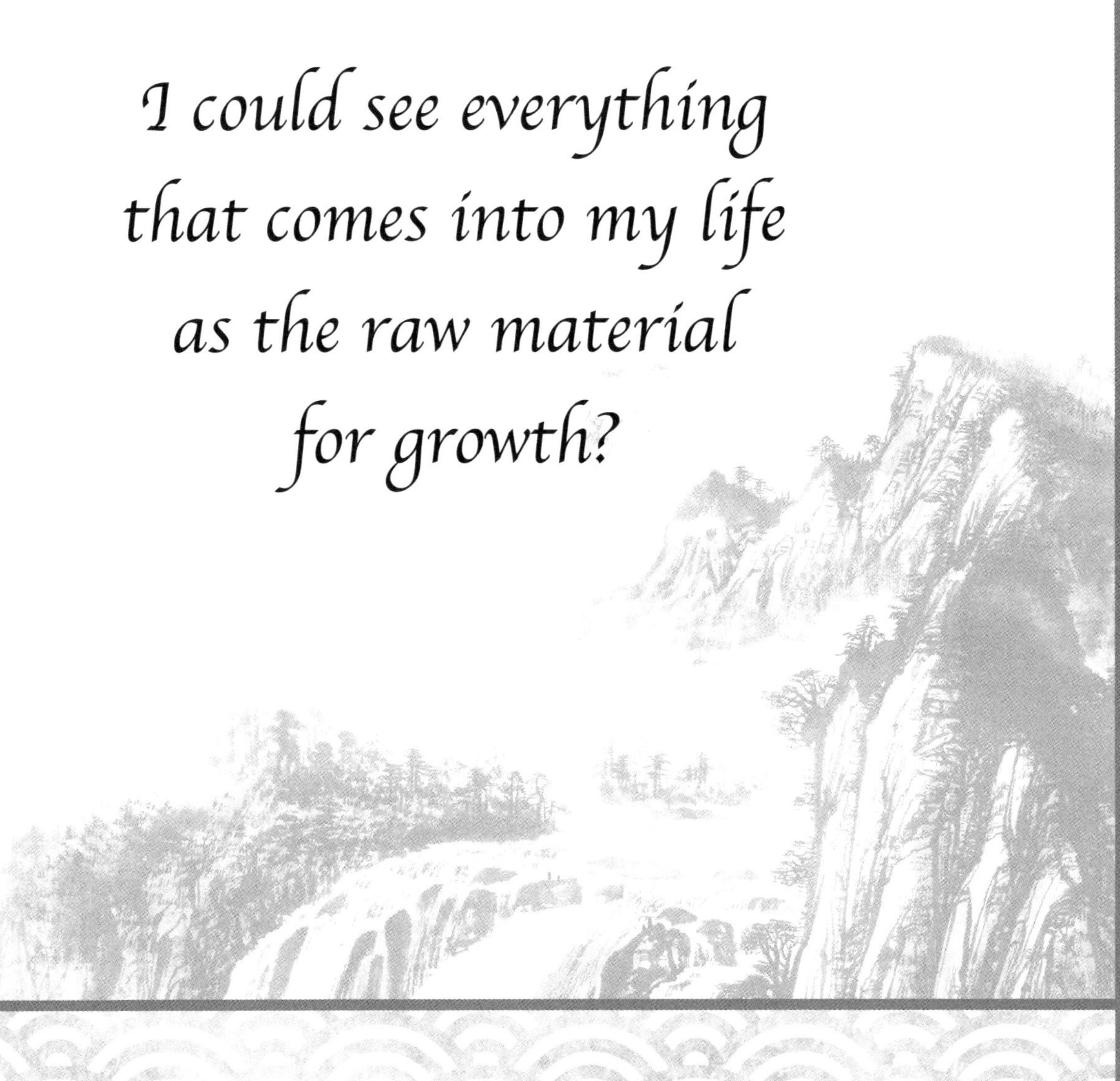

WHAT IF...

it is possible
to turn regrets
into useful insights
that benefit me and others?

WHAT IF...

circumstances do not need
to change in order
for new possibilities
to emerge?

WHAT IF…

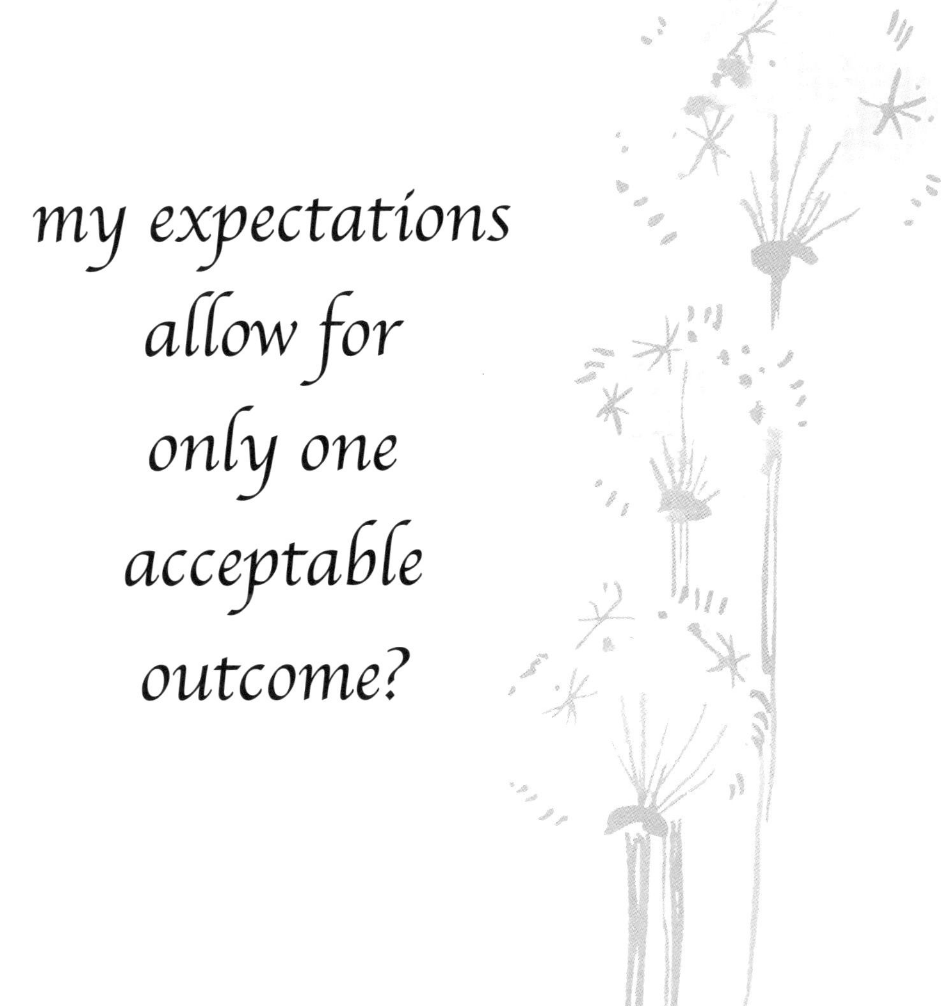

my expectations
allow for
only one
acceptable
outcome?

WHAT IF…

it is sometimes easier to forgive others than to forgive myself?

What If...

because I have lived
the world
will somehow
be different?

WHAT IF...

I trusted God's wisdom as much as I trust His power?

WHAT IF...

I really believed
every person has something
to teach me?

WHAT IF...

when "destroying darkness"
is my motivation,
I often destroy people
in the process?

WHAT IF...

I spent more time bringing healing to my relationships than trying to focus on who is to blame?

WHAT IF...

I am so at home
with myself
that I can be
"at home" anywhere,
with anyone?

WHAT IF...

I become so consumed
with the rush of life
that I end up with
a life filled with activity,
but experience nothing?

WHAT IF...

I took seriously the Bible's love chapter, 1 Corinthians 13 (MSG), that tells me that without love I am nothing but "the creaking of a rusty gate"?

WHAT IF...

we gave as much attention
to brain hygiene
as we do to body hygiene?

WHAT IF...

I spend more time learning the stories of celebrities than I do trying to understand my own story?

WHAT IF...

I learn to express caring in ways that foster growth rather than creating unhealthy dependency?

WHAT IF...

fear has the power to prevent me
from making decisions
that are in keeping with
what I believe and who I am?

What If…

God is more concerned with
the direction and focus
of my life than
He is with my
accomplishments?

WHAT IF...

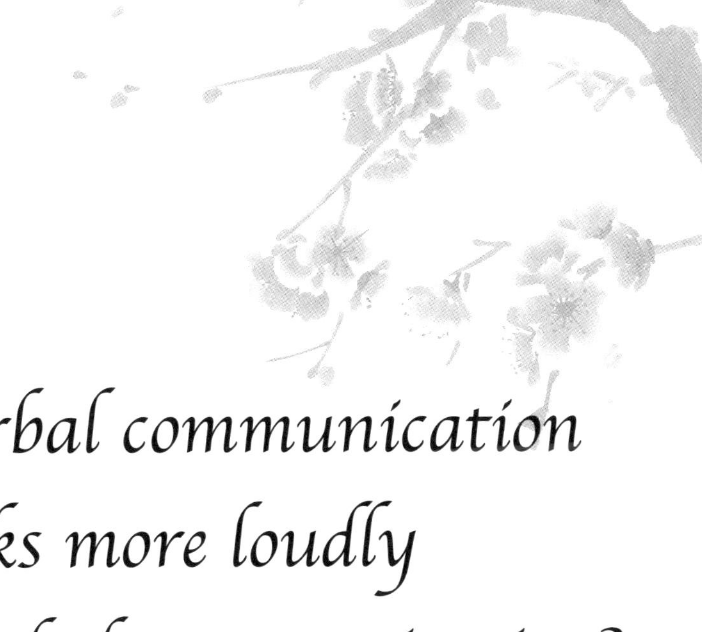

my nonverbal communication
speaks more loudly
than my verbal communication?

WHAT IF...

the reason I wound others
is because of my own
unhealed woundedness?

WHAT IF...

I have never identified what the "nonnegotiables" are in my life?

WHAT IF...

no matter how brief
or casual the contact,
we leave an imprint
on each other?

WHAT IF...

we are more afraid
of aging than dying?

WHAT IF...

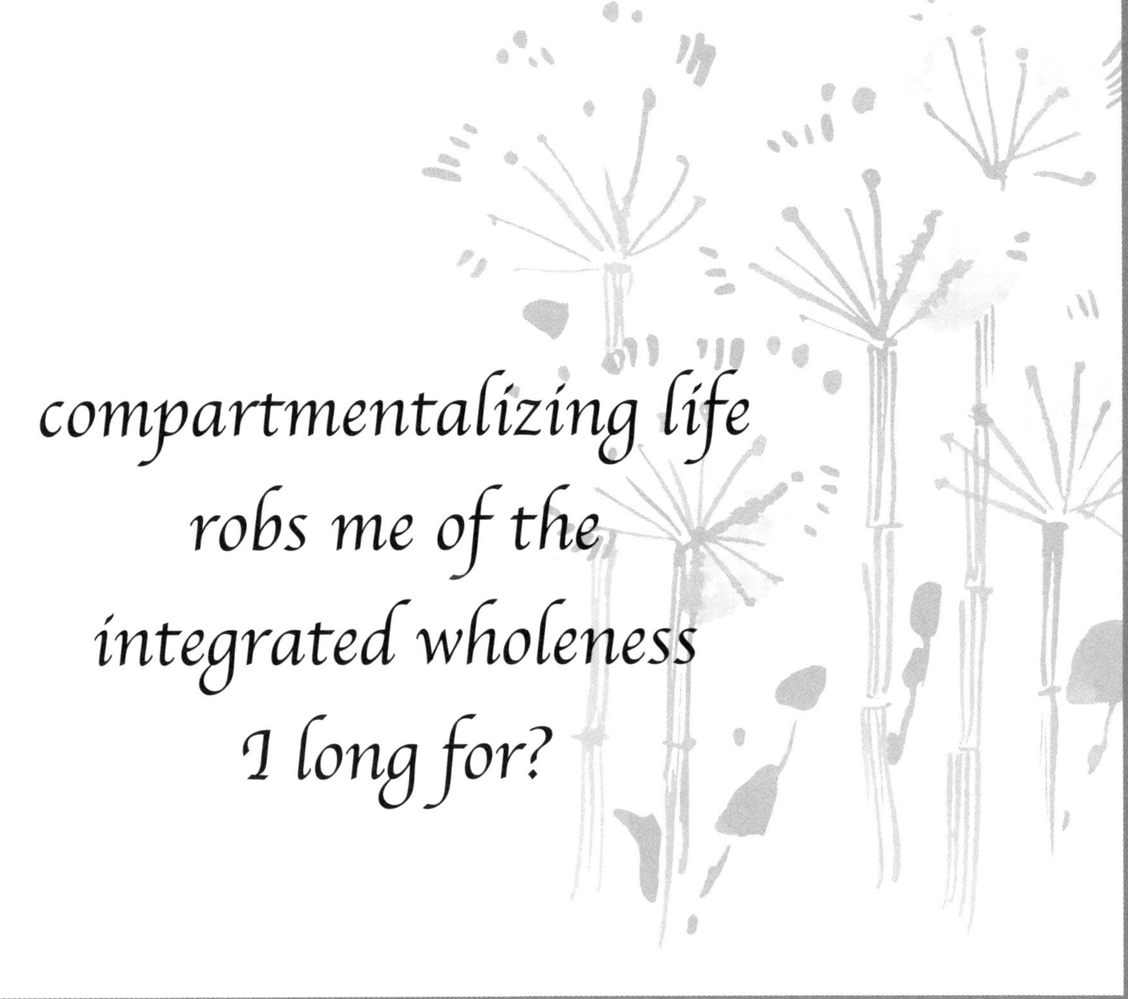

compartmentalizing life
robs me of the
integrated wholeness
I long for?

WHAT IF...

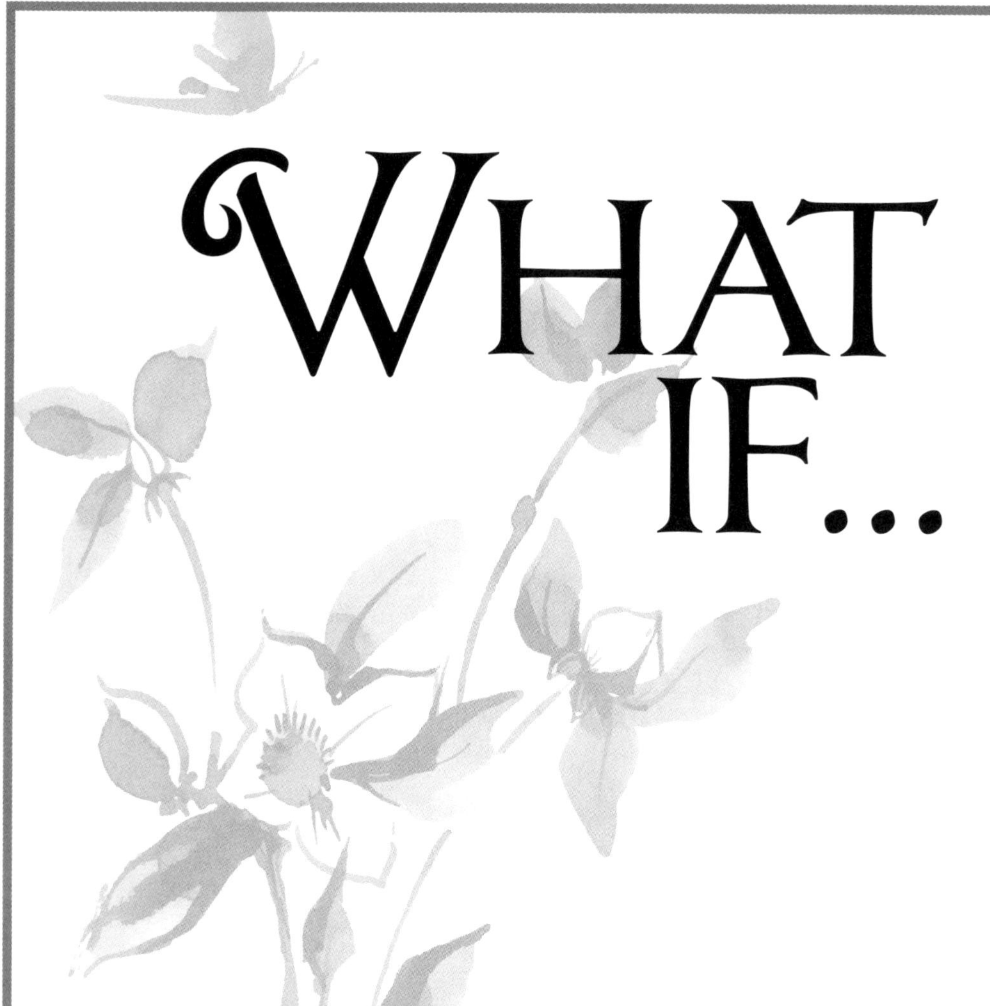

we could look beyond
outward appearance
and see every person
as a face of God?

WHAT IF...

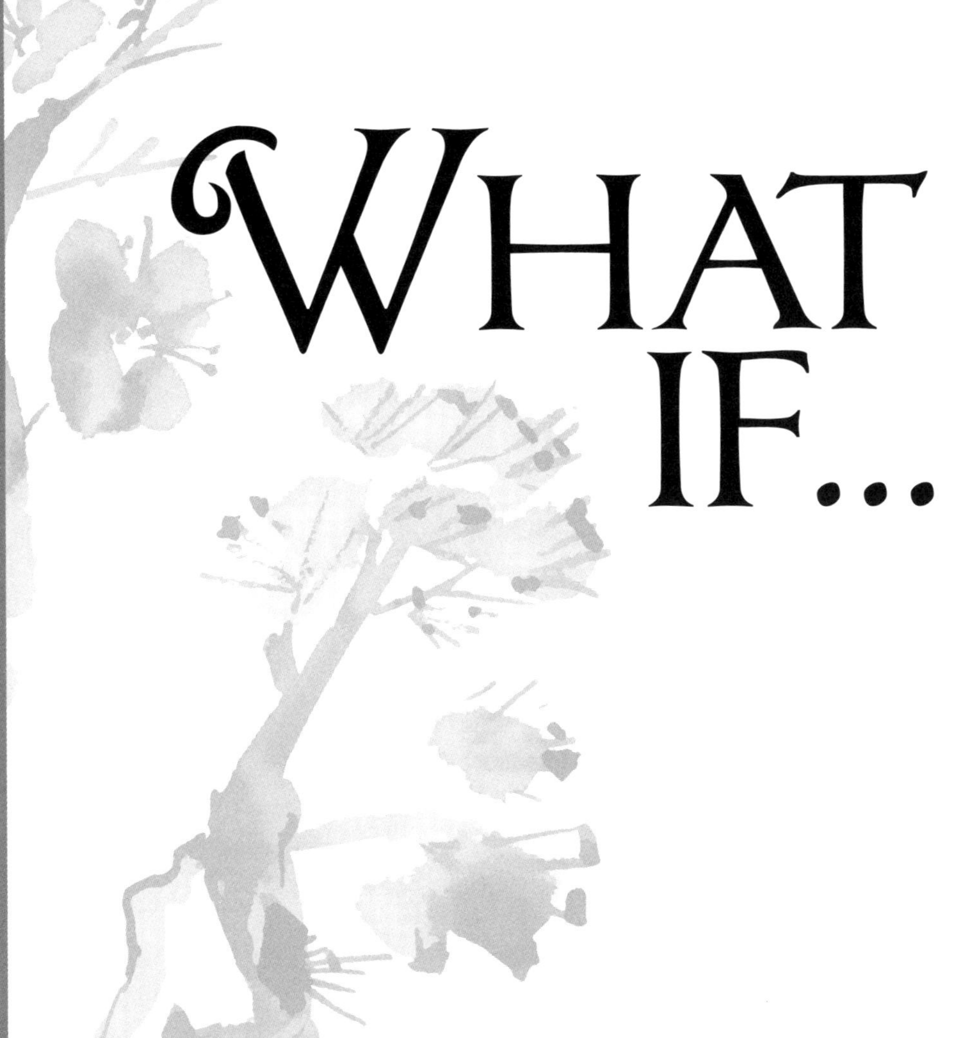

my story is not
about the facts
of my life,
but my experience
of those facts?

WHAT IF...

we teach people how to hide
unless we teach them
how to handle failures?

WHAT IF...

the blessings circling above my head
can find no place to land
because the runway of my life
is too crowded with expectations?

WHAT IF...

truly listening
is one of the greatest gifts
you can give
to another person?

WHAT IF...

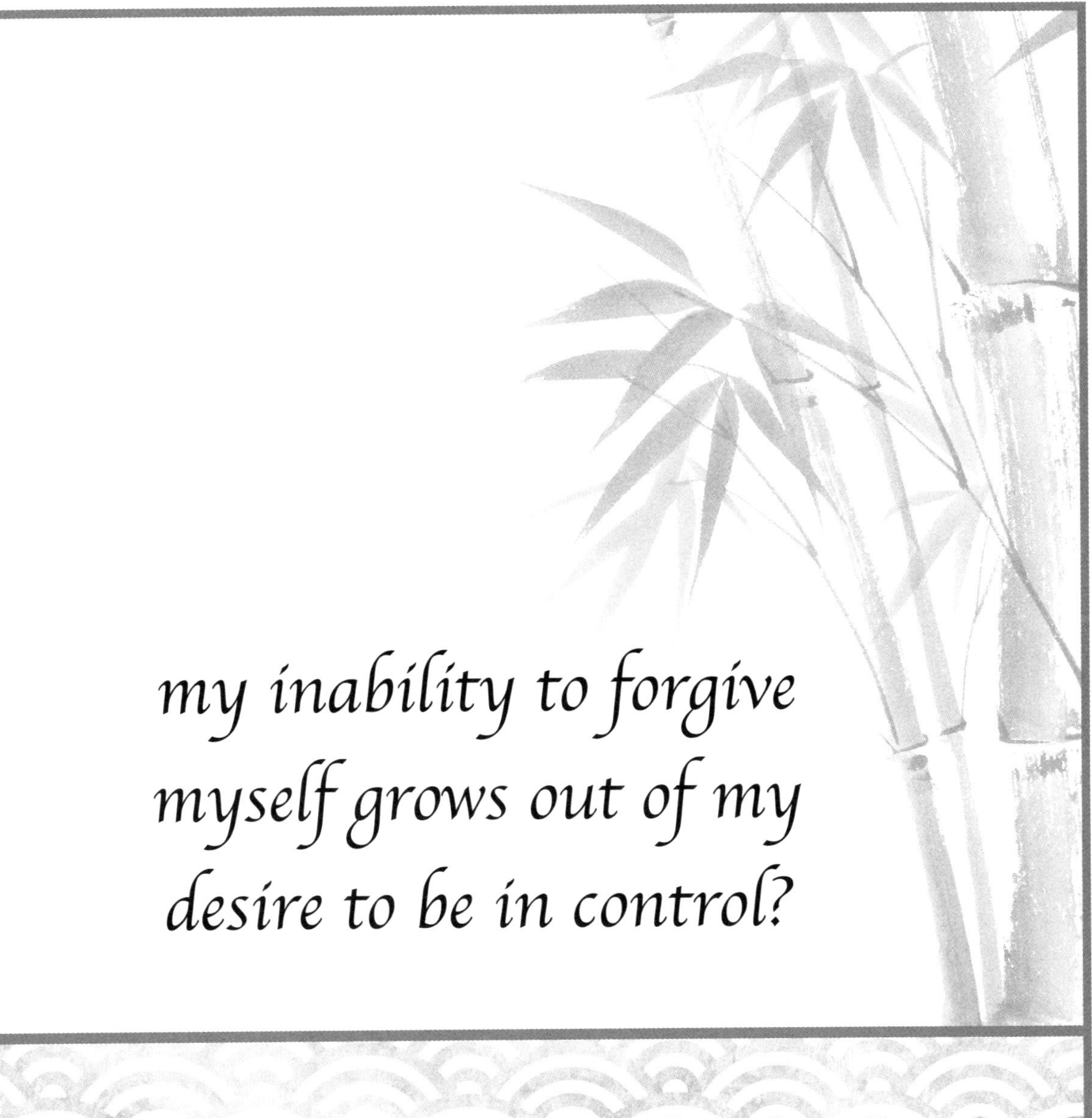

my inability to forgive
myself grows out of my
desire to be in control?

What If...

in my efforts to shut out
or avoid pain,
I shut out
the capacity to
experience joy?

WHAT IF...

I believed that perfect love
casts out fear and
that fear's control
lessens as love increases?

WHAT IF...

those who spend a lifetime
serving others are sometimes
the ones who find it
the most difficult to be served?

WHAT IF…

I wait to know the question before offering my thoughts?

WHAT IF...

I depended on
the eyes of my heart
more than my
physical eyes?

WHAT IF...

a wrong spirit can cancel the effectiveness of a right belief?

WHAT IF...

I stopped seeing certain people as irritations, interruptions, or roadblocks?

WHAT IF...

the way I relate
to others
prevents people
from seeing God
as a loving God?

WHAT IF...

I allow the labels I wear
or the titles I am given
to become my identity?

WHAT IF...

instead of seeking completion,
I need to seek wholeness?

WHAT IF...

because relationships
are messy and fluid,
I stopped trying to be
efficient and sought
to be effective?

What If...

I'm so obsessed with
"who I think I'm not"
that it hinders
who I can become?

WHAT IF...

I looked at my life as a story rather than a series of isolated events?

What If...

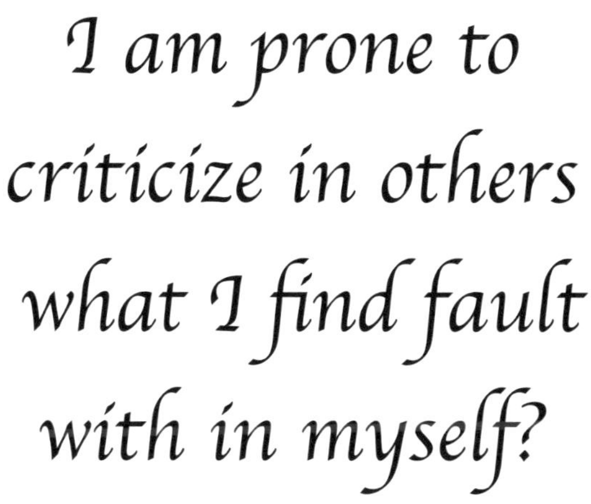

I am prone to criticize in others what I find fault with in myself?

WHAT IF...

I am more concerned about believing the right things than I am about following Jesus?

What If...

I turned my realities
into dreams
instead of trying
to turn unrealistic dreams
into reality?

WHAT IF...

there is no such thing
as a worthless person?

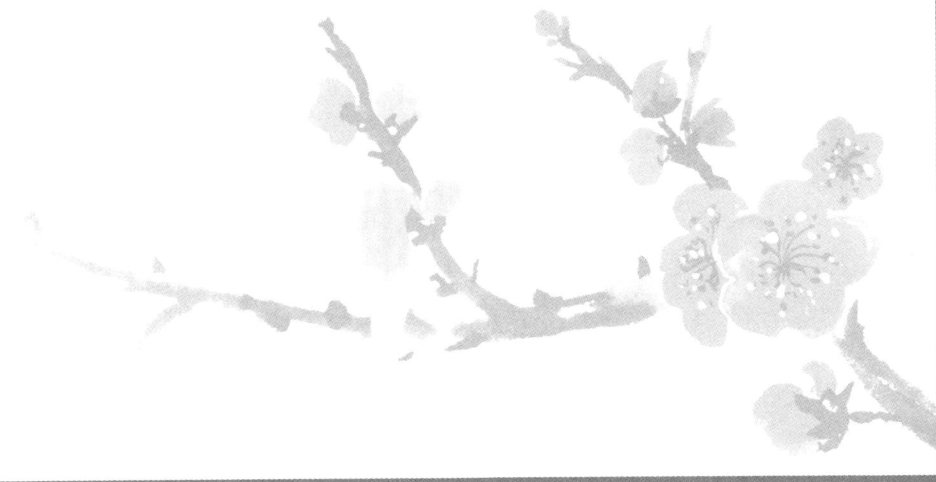

WHAT IF...

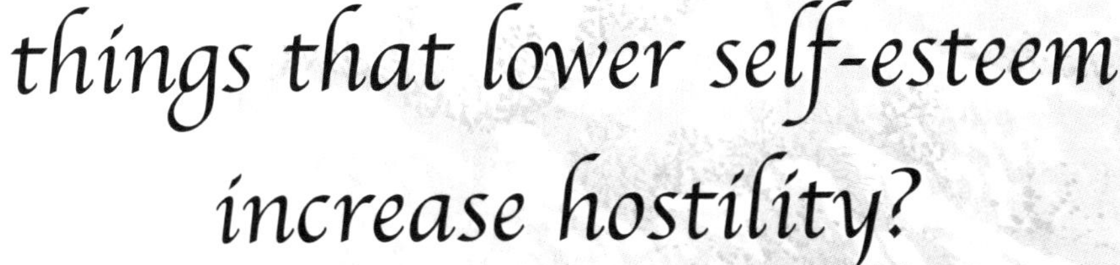

things that lower self-esteem
increase hostility?

WHAT IF...

it is not "when"
I learn something,
but "that" I learn it?

What if...

fear of loss causes me
to resist change?

WHAT IF...

there are miracles
all around me,
if only I had eyes
with which
to see them?

WHAT IF...

I faced my pain, loss, and grief by asking God to make them fruitful?

WHAT IF...

my need to belong can lead me
to become a part of something
that is harmful to me?

WHAT IF...

spoken words
are hard to forget?

WHAT IF...

I find it hard to rejoice with those who get something I wanted?

WHAT IF...

living in the
"if only" world
robs me of
the meaning
to be discovered
in the life I live?

WHAT IF...

I dared to allow
my true self
to be known?

WHAT IF...

hiding gets in the way of healing?

WHAT IF...

God is more concerned
with my spirit and attitude
than my beliefs?

What If...

in the aging process,
I allow my spirit to blossom
while my body deteriorates?

WHAT IF...

my unwillingness to forgive
is lethal to me,
but has little or
no effect on the person
I refuse to forgive?

What If...

boredom is a choice
as well as a condition?

WHAT IF...

I would be amazed
at what I am capable of
if I dared to risk finding out?

WHAT IF...

wishful thinking
is not the same
as hope?

What If...

I am so caught up and busy
doing good things
that I do not recognize
my lack of love?

WHAT IF...

gratitude changes life from endurance to adventure?

WHAT IF...

an overemphasis on self-care can result in self-indulgence?

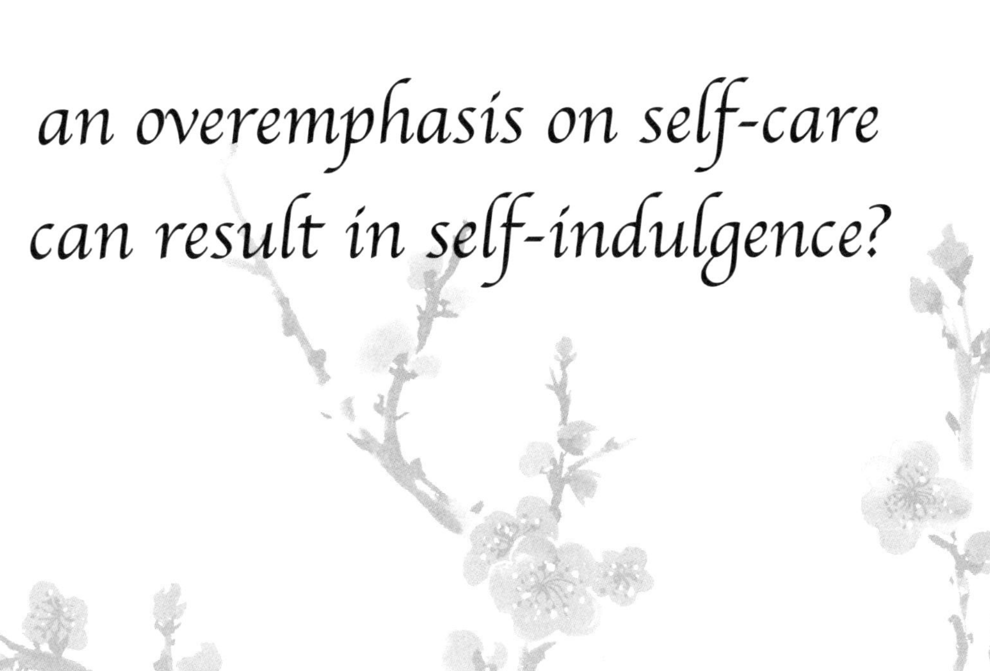

WHAT IF...

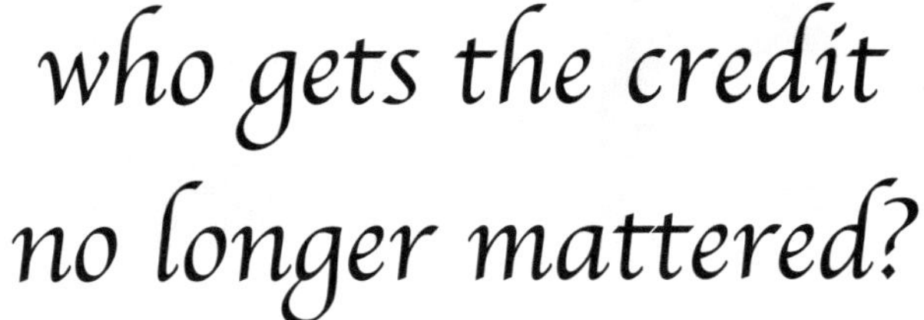

who gets the credit
no longer mattered?

WHAT IF...

instead of focusing on
solving problems and
resolving conflict,
I focused on helping people grow?

WHAT IF...

every person
is irreplaceable,
but no person
is indispensable?

WHAT IF...

I am so enslaved
to schedules
that I miss
a potentially incredible
interruption?

WHAT IF...

what I model is far more impactful than what I say?

WHAT IF...

awareness and amazement
are two things I need
to cultivate in my life?

WHAT IF...

appearances become more important than reality?

WHAT IF...

my life choices
reveal what
my values are?

WHAT IF...

I learned how to give people space to grow?

WHAT IF...

pain is a gift
because it
alerts us
that something
is wrong?

WHAT IF...

I am
my greatest
roadblock
to developing
a fulfilled life?

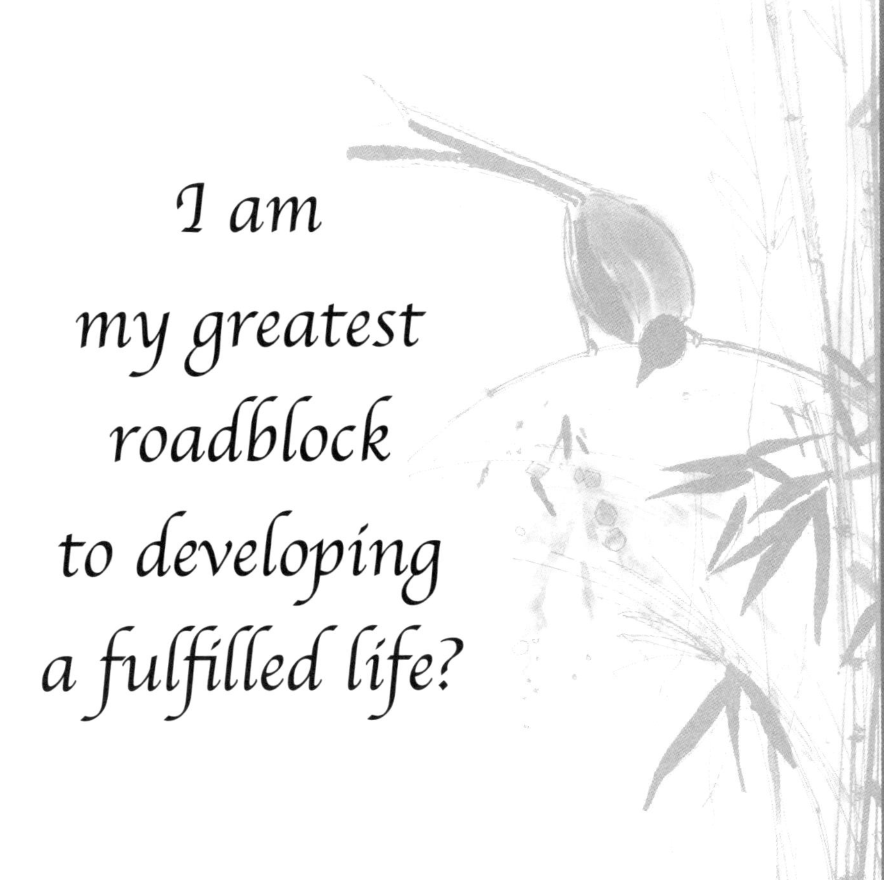

WHAT IF...

resentment is the result of allowing myself to be absolutely convinced that I do not have a choice?

WHAT IF...

there is a deeper meaning
to my life than
I have yet discovered?

WHAT IF...

I started with people where they are, rather than where I wish they were?

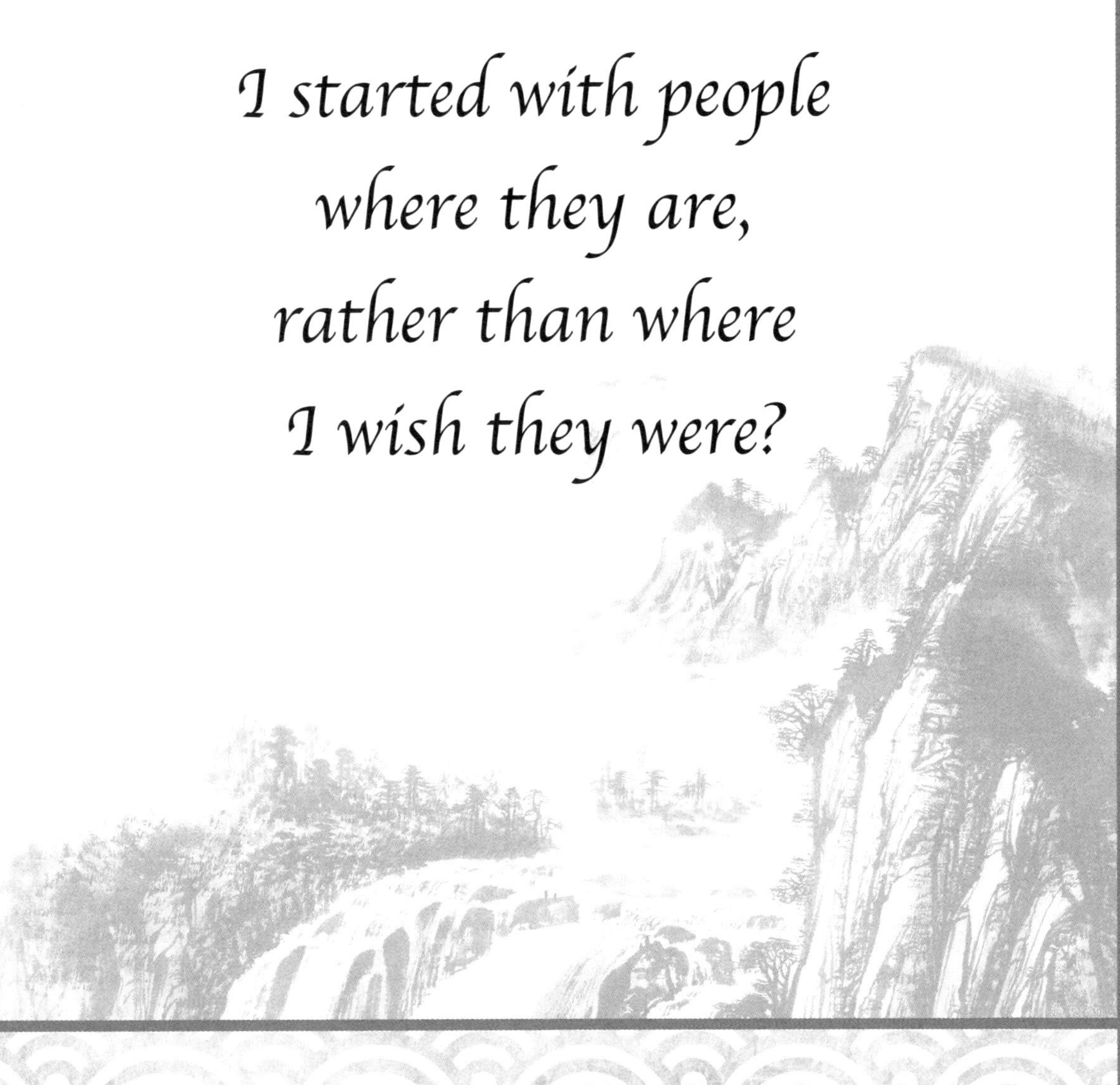

WHAT IF...

*love would make
us more relevant
than analyzing
and striving?*

WHAT IF...

I discovered that it is difficult, maybe impossible, to lead people I don't love and respect?

WHAT IF...

the idea that
"there are
no absolutes"
is an illusion?

WHAT IF...

there is grace
contained in
unanswered questions?

WHAT IF...

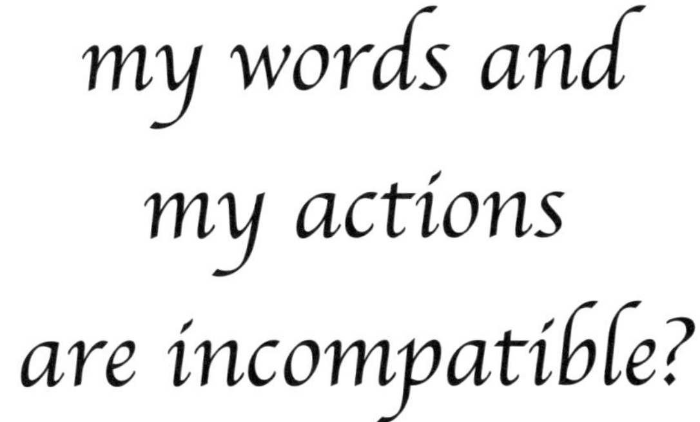

my words and
my actions
are incompatible?

WHAT IF...

learning from the past is essential, but living in the past is detrimental?

WHAT IF...

confused priorities
are hindering
my way forward?

WHAT
IF...

it is impossible
to not be shaped
by what I feed into my mind?

WHAT IF...

transparency is a must for building trust?

WHAT IF...

without honest questions,
I deprive myself
of the richness of life?

A Personal Note from the Author

Life is such a gift! I am so blessed that I have had the privilege of living a long life. Though it is a gift, it is not easy, but no matter how difficult it is, life always contains potential. I have found life to be an incredible teacher if I listen.

Questions have been an important nudge for me. They push me to reflect, to try to make sense out of the journey, to encourage me to become real, and drag me kicking and screaming to a place of honesty. Without questions, my life would have been far more just an existence rather than a life that greets each day with a sense of anticipation.

I have become keenly aware that nothing is original with me. The questions in this book came from something I heard, experienced, read, or came from God as I pondered. I believe that all truth comes from God, no matter through whom it comes.

Thanks be to God that people and all the different experiences of my life have caused questions to surface that have contributed to my growth. The exciting thing for me is that even at this stage of life, the questions keep on surfacing!

I also want to share with you that a portion of the proceeds from the sale of this book will go to an endowed scholarship fund for students, who without financial help, would not be able to attend my alma mater. My life was forever changed by attending Anderson University (anderson.edu), and I long for others to have the same opportunity.

I wish I could invite you to sit at my kitchen table in order to hear how you are processing the questions in your life. Remember, questions have a way of impacting you, one way or the other. You get to choose.